Original title:
Life: Where's My Instruction Manual?

Copyright © 2025 Creative Arts Management OÜ
All rights reserved.

Author: Nathaniel Blackwood
ISBN HARDBACK: 978-1-80566-153-5
ISBN PAPERBACK: 978-1-80566-448-2

## **Paths Woven with Threads of Hope**

Each morning I wake and check my phone,
If only it had answers, I wouldn't feel so alone.
With coffee in hand, I stumble to seek,
A map for my journey, but where's my cheat sheet?

Some days are smooth, like butter on toast,
Others feel like a game, and I'm not the host.
I laugh at the puzzles, the chaos and fun,
Navigating life, chasing a runaway sun.

## The Invisible Hands Guiding Us

I trip on my thoughts, they dance like my feet,
  Invisible forces keep me offbeat.
A nudge here, a shove there, I giggle and sway,
  Is it fate or just coffee that leads me astray?

In crowds I chat with the folks in my head,
  Imaginary wisdom I follow instead.
Who needs a GPS when a hunch is at play?
Taking the wrong turn can brighten the day!

## The Script We Write Together

We scribble our scripts in the sand by the shore,
Waves come and wash them, and we write some more.
With each silly blunder, a giggle escapes,
The plot thickens slowly, like soup with odd shapes.

Characters change like the seasons we greet,
With a wink and a nudge, we doodle our feet.
Adventures await in this jumbled refrain,
Penning a tale that's delightfully insane!

## **Between Each Breath, There Lies Wonder**

In the pause of a breath, a giggle is caught,
A tickle of joy in the mess I have fought.
With each little hiccup, I ponder and muse,
What's the next twist in my colorful blues?

The world spins around like a whirling top,
I chase after dreams that just dance and hop.
In moments of silence, the laughter pulls near,
Each breath is a treasure, let's toast with a cheer!

## The Enigma of Ordinary Days

What's that noise? My sock is missing!
Is it the dryer's secret mission?
Coffee spills become my art,
Each morning a brand new start.

Instructions lost in the pile,
Yet somehow I find my style.
Navigating this silly maze,
With laughter lighting up my days.

**Unlocking the Door of Experience**

Shall I dance on the dining room table?
Or attempt a new recipe with fable?
Each adventure a joyful surprise,
Just don't let the toast burn, wise guy!

Keys to wisdom in every misstep,
Like a cat that forgot how to prep.
Open the door, tread lightly, roam,
In the chaos, you might find home.

## Where Certainty Meets Chaos

They say the path is straight and narrow,
But I've taken a turn without a sparrow.
Juggling plans with glee and flares,
Unruly fate, grant me your prayers!

Nothing is certain, that's for sure,
Yet the unpredictability, I adore.
With laughter as my trusty guide,
I stumble through with arms open wide.

## The Art of Crafting Connections

Building bridges with a noodle and glue,
Strangers become friends with a quirky view.
Send a meme, share a laugh,
Crafty bonds make my heart dance and half.

In this tapestry of awkward chats,
We weave together like two goofing cats.
Each connection a thread in the quilt,
Where chaos thrives, fun is built.

## Wandering Through the Labyrinth

I took a turn, then another one,
Hoping to find a clue for fun.
My map was scribbled, a toddler's art,
Can someone please point me to the start?

I tripped on laughter, stepped on a joke,
Every twist was a riddle, not just smoke.
With every corner, a new surprise,
Running in circles, I lose track of time.

A Minotaur? Nah, just my lost sock,
It lost me first, what a tick-tock!
The path is jumbled, it's full of mirth,
In this maze of antics, I forgot my worth.

I laugh at the puzzle, embrace the jest,
Finding joy in chaos, I'm truly blessed.
As long as I wander, I'll stay light and free,
In a world that's crazy, that's the key for me.

## The Scribe of Unfinished Stories

I wrote a tale, halfway through,
The plot twisted, like spaghetti too!
Characters wandered, names come and go,
'Shall I have a cliffhanger?' No, just dough.

Pages crumbled, ideas flew,
An unfinished tale? Yeah, that's my crew.
They sip their coffee, looking so grim,
While I giggle at plots that are growing dim.

I launched a saga about a lost shoe,
How it escaped on the day it was due.
Chasing its partner, it jumped and it pranced,
A story in chaos, no chance for romance.

So here I sit, a scribe of glee,
With pens that run riot, and zero decree.
My laughter writes chapters, never a bore,
In this world of stories, there's always more.

## The Fortress of Unspoken Truths

Behind stone walls of quiet dread,
Lies a fortress where silence is fed.
Secrets linger like dust in the air,
Whispers want out, but I'm too aware.

Each brick I lay is a laugh in disguise,
Building my castle with fibs as my prize.
I'll host a banquet for truths that won't speak,
Each dish a giggle—a farcical leak!

My guards are clowns, oh what a sight,
Bouncing around, turning dark into light.
They juggle my worries, pass axes they throw,
In this fortress of fables, on laughter we grow.

So if you come knocking, bring jokes for the cheer,
We'll celebrate whispers with never a fear.
In my sturdy abode of humor and jest,
We'll feast on the funny—it's simply the best!

## **Collecting Moments, Not Directions**

I tossed my compass, pitched it away,
Directionless travel? Oh, what a play!
Every starlit path is a dance in disguise,
Collecting moments, much wiser am I.

With every pit stop, a memory blooms,
The car horn howls, then laughter consumes.
A detour to ice cream, then off to the zoo,
Why read the map when there's so much to do?

In a world of chaos, my heart finds the beat,
With spontaneous joy, I'm never discreet.
A giggle, a smile, each second's a gem,
Forget the directions, let's do it again!

A friend with a camera, we snap a few shots,
With silly poses and misplaced thoughts.
Every moment we gather is better than gold,
In this madcap adventure, it never gets old.

## **The Language of Stumbles**

I tripped over my shoes today,
A dance of chaos, come what may.
Instructions lost, but laughter found,
In every tumble, joy is crowned.

Maps are scribbles on a napkin,
Directions change like a chubby grin.
Follow the squirrel, take the leap,
If you fall, do it with style, don't weep.

I asked my cat for wisdom's glee,
She just yawned and stared at me.
Paw prints scattered, what's the plan?
Life's manual? Just chase the can!

So here's the key to endless glee,
Wobble, fumble, oh let it be!
In every flub, there's fun to find,
So laugh it off, and don't be blind.

## Lessons from the Uncharted

Set sail for shores unknown and wide,
With a snack in hand, and snacks to bide.
No compass here, just happy trails,
And the wind's whisper in our sails.

Maps appear like an unruly jigsaw,
Twisting routes that make you guffaw.
Take the left where the chickens cross,
Who knows? You might find a boss!

With each adventure, mix and stir,
A splash of chaos, a hint of blur.
Chart your course with jelly beans,
Life's sweeter when it's not so mean!

Oven mitts cannot save the day,
When you bake while dancing, hey, hooray!
Burned edges, but hear the cheer,
Lessons learned, we persevere!

## The Riddle of Curved Roads

Bumps and turns, mystery unwraps,
My GPS has lost its maps.
Follow the duck that waddles along,
Turns out wrong paths can feel quite strong.

Curvy roads like life's best jokes,
Each twist and turn, a laugh evokes.
Take the shortcut, oh wait, a wall,
Giggling as I prepare to fall.

Signs that say 'detour ahead',
Who knew they'd lead to a cozy bed?
Take a nap, the world can wait,
Sometimes slow is simply great.

An endless ride with silly friends,
Where the laughter spills and never ends.
So if you're stuck, let out a cheer,
For a wild ride brings joy so near!

## Recipes for the Heart's Journey

Ingredients of joy, a dash of strife,
Mix with giggles, that's the spice of life.
A sprinkle of hope, a cup of dreams,
Bake at warmth, watch love's beams.

Stir in chances, whisk in delight,
Add a pinch of courage, make it bright.
Follow the taste of what feels right,
When all else fails, just share a bite.

Chop up challenges, sauté them with ease,
Serve on a plate, passed with a tease.
Taste the mess, let flavors collide,
For laughter is the best along for the ride!

So whip it up with a gleeful grin,
Embrace the chaos, let the fun begin.
For each recipe shared, each heart will grow,
In this kitchen of dreams, let the love flow!

## Weaving Patterns of Dust and Dreams

In a world spun with threads so fine,
I lost my map, forgot the line.
Stumbling 'round like a dizzy fly,
Where's my guide? Oh me, oh my!

The coffee spills, the toast is burnt,
Lessons learned, yet still I yearn.
Between the giggles, falls, and grace,
I fumble on, still finding my place.

**The Archive of Each New Dawn**

Morning breaks, I hit snooze one more,
Dreaming of answers behind closed doors.
The sun peeks in with a cheeky grin,
Reminding me where mischief begins.

With each sunrise, a fresh to-do,
I scribble notes, but lose my shoe.
A giggle here, a snort somewhere,
I'll document it all – if I dare!

## Facets of Experience, Shining Bright

Each choice I make feels like a spin,
A carnival ride, let the chaos begin.
With gleaming hopes like balloons in the air,
I launch them high, forgetting my care.

From messy hair to mismatched socks,
I dance through life in a box of clocks.
Tick tock, the moments flee,
But laughter echoes, so wild and free.

## Glimmers in the Unfamiliar Ash

In the rubble, I search for gold,
Finding laughter where stories unfold.
Each trip and fall, a lesson learned,
Through trials and errors, my spirit burned.

As I sift through the dusty remains,
I spot the glimmers amidst the pains.
With winks and chuckles, I make my way,
Through the whispers of yesterday.

## Learning to Dance in the Dark

Stumbling like a newborn deer,
In a room that's full of cheer.
Twist and turn, what's that appeal?
My two left feet just missed the wheel.

Laughter echoes off the walls,
As I trip and make my falls.
Spinning wildly, hear me squeak,
Who turned off the lights this week?

I follow moves I cannot see,
A dance of pure calamity.
With every step, my balance gone,
I'm finding rhythm in the yawn.

Yet here I sway, a crazy sight,
In the dark, I dance with fright.
With each misstep, I find my tone,
Who needs a manual when you're alone?

## Echoes of a Forgotten Guide

Once I had a manual blue,
Filled with wisdom, tried and true.
Pages gone, it slipped away,
Now I fumble through the fray.

"Do this, don't do that," it said,
Now I'm lost, and full of dread.
I scribbled notes in crayon bright,
Chasing answers through the night.

"I should have listened," I now sigh,
But how to learn when I just fly?
Echoes of those words I heard,
Faltered truths are so absurd.

So here I stand, adrift, confused,
In this maze, I'm surely bruised.
Yet laughter bubbles, I can't deny,
In this folly, I'll still fly high!

## In Search of the Invisible Script

Wandering paths without a map,
I fumble through the funny gap.
What's the next step? Who can tell?
Is there a plot? I cannot gel.

I asked the stars for a script so clear,
But all I got was a cosmic sneer.
"Figure it out, you have some wit!"
Was that advice or just some grit?

With each twist and turn I make,
I wonder if there's a hidden stake.
A secret code, a whispered tale,
I'm chasing clues through fog and hail.

Yet still I dance and dodge the fate,
With laughter bubbling, it's first-rate.
In this crazy, wild little trip,
I write the lines without a script!

## Chasing Shadows of Certainty

Chasing shadows down a lane,
Where certainty is often vain.
I grab for truths that slip away,
Like ice cream cones on a hot day.

Questions fly like birds in spring,
Searching for that perfect ring.
But every answer leads to more,
A door that opens—what's in store?

I trip on jokes and puns galore,
Finding answers, but not a score.
Every turn brings comic flair,
Unraveling wisdom from thin air.

So let's embrace this wobbly chase,
With laughter lighting up the space.
In this game, we dance and spin,
The fun of search, that's where we win!

## The Vocabulary of Wanderlust

I packed my bags with all my dreams,
But forgot the maps, or so it seems.
A suitcase full of silly whims,
And yet I float on hopeful beams.

With each new turn, I pause and stare,
At signs that twist beyond compare.
What's left and right? It's hard to share,
Do carousels come with some flair?

I'll chase the view, but still get lost,
A detour here, it's worth the cost.
Where's the guide for this wild froth?
I swear, there's gold under the moss!

But here I am, a traveler bold,
With stories wrapped in laughter's fold.
So let's toast to misadventures told,
And wander free, like we were sold!

## Poetic Frustrations of a Navigator

A compass spins, a clock unwinds,
The stars are shy, no one aligns.
I'm charting signs with crayon lines,
Why can't I find the place that shines?

With cada paso, I lose my way,
A laugh or two can make my day.
What does the GPS even say?
A riddle wrapped in disarray!

My maps are drawn in doodles bright,
Hoping to quell this inner fright.
I'll sail the seas or take to flight,
But wait—did I leave on the right?

So arm me well with snacks and glee,
We'll wander off, just you and me.
These misdirections, oh, the spree!
What joy it is just to be free!

## Shadows of Tips and Tricks

In shadows cast by wisdom's glow,
I seek the shortcuts I don't know.
A tip for tea, a trick for snow,
But all I find is quite the show.

I ask the wise for pearls of thought,
But muddled riddles are what I've caught.
With every clue, more fact is fought,
It's like a stew of wisdom's pot.

So where's the handbook for this game?
Do I just laugh or go insane?
With quirks and quirks, it's all the same,
Dancing in circles, never tame.

Yet here we stand, with heart so light,
Through all the chaos, taking flight.
I'll drop my notes, embrace the night,
And turn these shadows into bright!

## Deciphering the Enigma of Being

There's no decoder for this plight,
I twist and turn, yet seek the light.
A riddle wrapped in pure delight,
Why's this journey feeling tight?

With every step, I scratch my head,
And wonder what the wise have said.
They scribble notes while I'm misled,
On coffee cups where dreams are fed.

I juggle plans like pesky fruit,
A bumbling clown in a cute suit.
My path is wild, and that's the root,
Should I sing loud or just dispute?

But joy is found in every glance,
In silly falls and awkward dance.
So here we are—let's take a chance,
Embrace the mess, it's our romance!

## Recipes for the Unknown

Take a pinch of joy, sprinkle with doubt,
Mix in some chaos, but leave room to shout.
Simmer on low when the questions arise,
Serve with a side of hilarious surprise.

For every recipe, a dash of the strange,
Garnish with laughter, allow for change.
Ignore the reviews, trust your own taste,
In this quirky kitchen, there's no time to waste.

Grab a spoonful of dreams, just let them swirl,
Fry failures crisp till they twirl and whirl.
Trust your instincts, a pinch of delight,
This unpredictable feast makes everything right.

In this bizarre banquet where no one's a pro,
Eating your mistakes, just let them flow.
No need for a manual, just laugh and believe,
In this wild restaurant, you learn how to weave.

## The Unfolding Script of Daydreams

I wrote my script in the coffee's steam,
Plot twists appear, or so it would seem.
Characters stumble on paths so absurd,
I giggle at plots never quite heard.

The hero forgot all his lines that day,
And lost in the forest, he wandered away.
The villain was busy with snacks and a drink,
Oh, what a tale that makes you rethink.

Scenes change with breezes that tickle my nose,
My stories sprout legs, while I just doze.
The script on the table is messy and torn,
Yet from these odd scribbles, new dreams are born.

Forget the mistakes; just roll with the flow,
Improvise freely, let imagination grow.
In this theater of dreams, no worries take flight,
Laughter and whimsy make everything bright.

## Crafting Narratives from Fragments

I found a sock, and it whispered a tale,
Of laundry mischief and socks gone pale.
With buttons for characters and lint in the mix,
I penned a short story, out of cheap tricks.

Fragments of moments are scattered like leaves,
Each one a story where laughter weaves.
The missing shoe held a party last night,
Inviting the dust bunnies, what a great sight!

Old newspapers tell of mishaps and scores,
Of heroic pets and mischievous chores.
I gather them up, these quirky old finds,
And weave them together, as laughter unwinds.

So here's to the puzzle, this jumbled delight,
Where nothing is perfect yet everything's right.
In crafting these snippets, I've found that it's true,
The joy of the journey's the best part of you.

## Muse of the Mishap

Oh, dear muse, of blunders and slips,
You dance among chaos, and giggles eclipse.
With each little fumble and twist of my fate,
You sprinkle on joy, never leave it too late.

The paint spills, and suddenly it's art,
A masterpiece born from a whole world apart.
With a wink and a grin, you guide my way,
Turning nightmares to punchlines, in bright shades of gray.

Trip on the sidewalk, then shake it off quick,
Life's greatest moments arrive with a flick.
In every misstep, a story does bloom,
In this funny little world, there's always more room.

So let us embrace every stumble and fall,
With laughter as glue, we'll conquer them all.
For in this sweet chaos, my muse finds her chat,
The mishaps are treasures, and oh, how they splat!

## The Palette of Uncertain Colors


With crayons and markers, I scribble a plan,
But chaos erupts, it's not going as planned.
Colors collide in a vibrant array,
Who knew that blue could get lost in the gray?

The paint can spills, a rainbow cascades,
I laugh at the mess and my vibrant charades.
Each stroke a riddle, each splash a surprise,
In this artwork of life, I blur with the skies.

What am I painting? A castle or frog?
Sometimes it's a key, sometimes just a fog.
I grin at the canvas, the absurdities flow,
This masterpiece makes me feel all aglow.

So let's embrace colors, both wild and bizarre,
In the end, it's a journey, not a race to a star.
For every mishap, I'll raise up a toast,
To the palette of life, where we laugh the most!

## The Footnotes of Forgotten Tales

In a dusty old book, where stories reside,
Footnotes are whispers of dreams left aside.
Each tale's got a quirk, like socks without pairs,
A knight on a cat with outrageous hair.

A napping princess in a castle of cheese,
Wakes up for a snack, completely at ease.
The dragon's a couch, the quest's just a game,
With heroic efforts to find his own name.

With every new chapter, the plot takes a twist,
Heroes get sidetracked, by breakfast, they missed.
Yet laughter's the compass, the guide for the roam,
In footnotes of stories, we find our own home.

So pen down your fables, let your laughter ring,
For life's just a tale, where we all are the king.
In the margins, we'll dance, and create our own lore,
With footnotes of humor, forever explore!

## Rewriting the Narrative of Being

I woke up one morning, feeling quite grand,
But the coffee was cold; nothing went as planned.
Scripted adventures turn into a farce,
As I trip on my dreams and land on the stars.

My to-do list vanished, it ran off in fright,
Now I nap like a champion, feeling just right.
Each mishap's a chapter in a book of delight,
Where clumsy and quirky are always in sight.

I'm rewriting my story with each silly mistake,
Embracing the moments, the laughter they make.
So here's to the fumbles, the stumbles, the falls,
They add up to wisdom; they dance on the walls.

With joy as my pen, and humor my guide,
I'll scribble my saga on this wobbly ride.
For living's an authoring, a mess we all share,
In the narrative of being, we're all debonair!

# Threads of Destiny's Tapestry

I weave through the day with mismatched thread,
Stitching up dreams, but they're hanging by thread.
My tapestry's quirky, with patches of fun,
Each knot tells a story of battles I've won.

The loom's gone haywire, but I don't really care,
Every twist in the fabric is woven with flair.
From sunflowers spinning to dragons in flight,
This colorful chaos brings pure delight.

With needles that jiggle and laughter that sings,
I craft my existence from shiny, weird things.
Unraveled, re-knotted, let's dance in the fray,
For threads of a tapestry are here just to play.

So gather your snippets and join in the game,
In the workshop of fate, life's never the same.
With every odd loop, we charm and we cheer,
In the tapestry of nonsense, hilarity's near!

## Lessons Hidden in the Breeze

I wandered through a field of thoughts,
Chasing butterflies with tangled knots.
The sun was bright, my shoes were lost,
Who knew fun would come at such a cost?

I tried to ask a tree for tips,
But it just stood there, full of quirks.
The flowers giggled, petals swayed,
As if to say, 'This mess you made!'

The breeze, it whispered secrets near,
Like how to live with grin and cheer.
Yet I tripped on roots, fell to the ground,
And laughed out loud at what I found.

In every tumble, every flight,
There's wisdom wrapped in sheer delight.
So I'll embrace the chaos, see,
For moments lost are moments free.

## A Compass Made of Questions

With a compass spinning in my hand,
I set out on a quest so grand.
But north kept laughing, running away,
Was my map made of cheese? No way!

I asked a squirrel where to go,
It pointed up, 'Just say hello!'
To clouds above, to ants below,
My compass now was in for a show.

Each question spun a wild new thread,
What to eat or where to tread?
A riddle formed in every glance,
I tripped and fell, but took a chance.

Through every twist, my heart did race,
For finding fun is the best embrace.
So here I stand, no plans in sight,
Just joy in searching, pure delight.

## Scribbles in the Margins of Existence

I found a book with pages blank,
Full of scribbles, a messy prank.
"Here's where I lost my keys," I wrote,
And "Dinner's burned!" in all caps, quote.

In margins wide, a laugh or two,
"Remember the time we fell in goo?"
Sticky stories, mismatched socks,
A life of puzzles in jumbled blocks.

I doodled hopes next to my dreams,
And painted woes with rainbow beams.
Each tear and giggle left a trace,
In this quirky, wondrous space.

So grab a pen, make your own mess,
For in the chaos lies true success.
With every page that bends and creases,
You'll find the joy that never ceases.

## Echoes of Unanswered Queries

Why do ducks walk in a line?
And why is it that clocks don't whine?
Questions bounce off walls, so loud,
I giggle softly, feeling proud.

An owl hoots back, a wise old tease,
While raindrops dance like they're at ease.
Each echo answers more than we think,
Like "What if the soda's made me pink?"

In every question, a smile hides,
Through riddle and jest, true wisdom glides.
Like why do people trip in jest?
Maybe it's all a hilarious test!

So here's to the queries that fill our days,
In their silliness, joy always stays.
With laughter ringing like sweet chimes,
Let's cherish the echoes, in our rhymes.

## The Art of Making Mistakes

In the kitchen, flour flies,
Eggs scrambled, oh what a surprise!
A cake that tastes just like a shoe,
But hey, who needs a recipe that's true?

With every trip and every fall,
I laugh aloud, I heed the call.
A life of blunders, some would say,
The mess I make, my own ballet!

## Scribbles in the Margins of Time

Amid the pages, notes and doodles,
My thoughts escape like playful poodles.
I ponder grand plans in messy ink,
Then spill my coffee, oh, what do you think?

Life's a book with unstamped stamps,
Each moment scribbled in time's cramp.
With lines that wiggle and twist just so,
I search for wisdom in the overflow.

## **Unfolding the Unknown Chapters**

I turn the page, what's this surprise?
A new plot twist, oh my, oh my!
With every chapter, I cringe and chuckle,
Unraveling truths, but still in a muddle.

Lost in stories of all my woes,
In the margins, laughter grows.
Each error a tale, each giggle a page,
I dance through the chaos, my witty age!

## The Puzzle of Everyday Moments

Pieces scattered, where does this go?
The coffee spills, the cat steals the show.
A jog that turns into a stroll,
Searching for socks—oh, that's my goal!

Puzzles form with quirks and laughs,
The joy I find in odd little gaffes.
In every mix-up, there's a piece so grand,
Embracing the chaos, I take a stand!

## Finding Wisdom in the Wilderness

I wandered in the woods one day,
Chasing shadows and light at play.
A squirrel shouted, "What's the plan?"
I shrugged and said, "I'm just a fan!"

Through tangled vines and leaves I tripped,
My hopes and dreams all tightly gripped.
A wise old tree imitated my fall,
Reminding me: it's fine to sprawl!

A rabbit laughed, pointed with glee,
"You think you're lost; just follow me!"
Turns out GPS is in their ears,
But I just brought snacks and a few beers!

In this maze of bushes, I found a way,
To dance with chaos, come what may.
No manual's needed to embrace the thrill,
Just a sense of humor, and a decent will!

## The Art of Unscripted Journeys

I hopped on a train with no ticket in hand,
Exploring the world, it was truly grand.
The conductor yelled, "Hey, where to?"
I grinned and replied, "It's a surprise for you!"

Maps folded up, lost in my bag,
I stepped out of bounds, what a zigzag!
A parrot squawked, "You're off the track!"
I shrugged and replied, "No looking back!"

Through winding roads and sleepy lanes,
Each detour filled with joys, not pains.
An ice cream truck sold wisdom too,
"Every scoop adds flavor, that's my cue!"

So I wandered on, laughter my guide,
No rulebook needed for this wild ride.
In unscripted paths, I found my way,
Life's hiccups are just the price we pay!

## **Pages of Unexplored Paths**

I opened a book with blank pages wide,
Took a pen, and let my thoughts slide.
"Where's chapter one?" I pondered in jest,
A dog barked, "Just write, you're blessed!"

Each sentence wobbled like jelly on toast,
Characters mingled, I loved them the most.
A cat intervened, said, "What's the plot?"
I laughed and confessed, "I've got naught!"

Through paragraphs thick, I stumbled and swayed,
Plot twists emerged, and plans mislaid.
But every mishap became a new line,
A rollicking rhyme found in good time!

So here in my tale, I've learned to embrace,
The chaos of ink in an unwritten space.
With each wavering line, a story unfolds,
In pages uncharted, my path is retold!

## The Manual of Missteps

Once I found a manual bound in red,
Thought I'd crack it, get ahead!
But inside was nothing but a bowl of soup,
"Instructions unclear, just jump through hoops!"

With mishaps galore, I'd often flop,
Tripped on my dreams; never could stop.
A slip on a banana was quite a scream,
"This might be a chapter, not part of my dream!"

In the art of missteps, wisdom unfolds,
"Practice makes perfect!" as my mother told.
I wore my blunders like badges of pride,
Each hilarious fail turned the tide!

And now I embrace the quirks of my path,
With laughter and joy, I escape the wrath.
For no manual exists that fits everyone,
Just roll with the punches and have some fun!

## The Chronicles of Wandering Souls

In a world of odd directions,
We stumble, trip, and fall,
Like GPS with no connection,
We ask ourselves, 'What's the call?'

With maps drawn by a toddler,
We navigate a mess,
Each laugh is like a boulder,
But hey, who needs success?

The compass spins with glee,
While our shoes fill with mud,
We declare, 'We're wild and free!'
Life's more fun with a thud!

So here's to every blunder,
And each crazy twist of fate,
We'll wear our chaos like thunder,
And celebrate, never wait!

## Unpacking the Bag of Surprises

I opened my bag of tricks,
And found socks that don't pair,
A dancing frog that clicks,
And last week's lunch with air!

There's wisdom in the clutter,
Like chocolate after dinner,
Life's mysteries just mutter,
And I giggle, slight beginner.

Who needs a book of rules?
When my cat's the judge of fun,
They pounce on fated fools,
And end the day with sun!

So let's embrace the strange,
With mismatched socks and glee,
Each pack is just a change,
Of how I see the spree!

## Scripting my Story in Sand

With each wave, my words dissolve,
Like ice cream on a cone,
I scribble lines that evolve,
Yet somehow feel like home.

The seagulls shout, "You're a joke!"
While I smile at the chaos,
As grains of fate lightly poke,
I wonder who's the boss?

Footprints follow like bad rhymes,
But I dance upon the shore,
Each stumble yet unwinds,
A little laugh, and oh, encore!

So here I stand, unshaken,
In the sand, my story's spun,
With giggles, dreams awakened,
Scripting fun has begun!

## Shadows Dancing with Destiny

My shadow's got some sass,
It creeps and crawls with flair,
Sometimes it trips on grass,
And tells me, 'Do beware!'

With moonlight as our DJ,
We tango 'round the trees,
Each twist is pure cliché,
Yet it whispers, 'Dance with ease!'

My destiny's a prankster,
It hides behind the sun,
But laughing gets much vaster,
When we both choose to run!

So let the shadows play,
In this silly masquerade,
With every wobbly sway,
I know joy will invade!

## **The Blueprint of Uncertainty**

I woke up this morning, what should I wear?
T-shirt, shorts, or maybe a bear?
I check the weather, it's sunny, then rain,
Oh, a map would help, but I'm just insane.

I follow the rules, but they twist and bend,
Like trying to make a break dance with a friend.
Every step chosen seems silly at best,
Perhaps I should ask a confused, clueless guest.

The path isn't clear, and that's quite alright,
I'll trip on my shoelace, but I'll stand up bright.
My GPS is broken, sent me to a mall,
Yet here I am laughing, I'm having a ball.

I'll craft my own guide, with laughs as my key,
A manual of chaos that sets my mind free.
Who needs directions when you've got a grin?
Just laugh at the chaos, let the fun begin!

## **Instructions Engraved in Stars**

I peek at the sky, looks like a mess,
A cosmic map scribbled, no time to guess.
Stars dance in patterns, or so they declare,
But which way to go? Oh, I'm pulling my hair!

Constellations whisper, 'It's all just a game,'
Or maybe it's just they're playing with fame.
I follow Orion, but he's out for a stroll,
And the Big Dipper? Well, it's lost its role.

A comet flies past, leaving trails in the night,
I'll catch it and ride, it might be a flight!
Instructions in stardust, what a curious plot,
I'll make it my guide, in the end, what have I got?

So here in the dark, I'll chart my own way,
With space as my mentor, I'll dance and I'll sway.
Even if I'm lost in the vast, rolling sea,
The stars say, 'Just smile! It's your journey, be free!'

## The Journey Through Uncharted Waters

I set sail today, on a boat made of dreams,
With paddles of laughter and sails of sweet cream.
The map has a coffee stain, oh what a sight,
But I'm ready for waves, for a splash or a bite!

The fish all are laughing, swimming in line,
While I try to steer, but I'm sipping on wine.
The compass spins wildly, it must think it's a game,
But that's half the fun, it's all part of the fame.

Clouds up ahead look like fluffy white pies,
I wonder if I could take a slice if I try.
Nautical nonsense? Oh, what's on the chart?
I'll navigate joy with my mix of pure art.

So here's to the journey, mishaps galore,
With a pinch of absurdity, I'll always explore.
With dolphins as guides and the sun as my cheer,
I'll sail through confusion, without any fear!

## **Whispers of Forgotten Teachings**

Old scrolls of wisdom turned brittle and gray,
Speak softly to me of a back-in-the-day.
But who can make sense of the scribbles and signs?
It's like trying to read riddles from silly designs.

"Don't touch that!" they shout from the echoes of years,
But I tend to giggle, I'll poke through the fears.
"Climb every mountain!" the shadows do croon,
Yet I trip on my shoelaces beneath the full moon.

I look for the teachers, but they're all on break,
With donuts and coffee, and 'give me a shake.'
I laugh with the ghosts, though they're not much help,
They mumble 'Just wing it!' with a cheeky yelp.

So onward I wander, with a wink and a grin,
What's lost in the lessons? Just let it begin!
I'll dance with confusion, my partner so bright,
In whispers of wisdom, I'll find my delight!

## Navigating the Unwritten Map

I took a step, then stumbled twice,
The map is blank, but that's quite nice.
The paths are wild, with twists and turns,
Yet every misstep, I live and learn.

With every fork, I flip a coin,
Decisions made in playful join.
A squirrel laughs, it seems to know,
While I just follow where the wind blows.

A sign appears, but it makes no sense,
"Beware of gnomes, it's quite intense!"
I chuckle softly, take a glance,
And join the gnomes for a merry dance.

Maps are for those who fear the ride,
I'll scribble my own and take it in stride.
For every wrong turn that I now embrace,
I find a new treasure, a smile on my face.

## The Rulebook of Breath

I sought a guide for how to be,
A manual lost, just like my key.
Do I inhale, exhale with flair?
Or dance around like I just don't care?

A chapter starts with things to fear,
But laughing out loud is all I hear.
Chapters on love are so absurd,
Find your own song, not just a word.

Footnotes take me down a road,
With puzzling fun that lightens the load.
To breathe is simple, who knew it could be?
I'll draft my own rules, and let my soul free.

The written pages look like a mess,
Filled with doodles, it's all a guess.
Yet in the chaos, I find my way,
It's all about the fun of today!

## Chasing Shadows Without Guides

I chase shadows on a funky trail,
With no compass, no map, just a playful pale.
Footprints wander without a plan,
Hopping like frogs, as only I can.

The sun's a joker, it hides and seeks,
While I follow giggles; adventure peaks.
Behind bushes, whispers swirl and scream,
In this crazy chase, I'm living the dream.

The shadows dance in a silly ballet,
They trip and tumble, leading the way.
With no GPS, I smile in glee,
For every wild turn sets my spirit free.

So here I am, a merry old fool,
Embracing the light with giggles as fuel.
With every misstep, I twirl and glide,
Chasing those shadows, a joyful ride!

## Threads of Chaos and Clarity

My life, a tapestry, frayed at the seams,
Woven with laughter, stitched up with dreams.
Colors collide in a playful swirl,
Dancing through chaos, watch my thread twirl.

Einstein said time is but a game,
Yet I'm just lost, feeling quite the same.
A needle here, a thimble there,
Sewing my hopes with the utmost care.

Stray strands tangle, what a lovely mess,
In this confusion, I learn to express.
With every knot that I find in the way,
I craft a new story for each bright day.

So here's my patchwork, imperfect and bold,
Each error a gem, each moment a gold.
In threads of chaos, clarity lights,
I'll laugh at my life and revel in flights!

## Whispers from the Unseen Pages

In a world of twists and turns,
I fumble like a duck that yearns.
Instructions lost, where did they go?
Guess I'll wing it, put on a show.

Cup spills coffee as plans go wrong,
My GPS sings a confusing song.
Pack your jokes and don your hat,
Life's a circus, and I'm the brat.

Chasing whispers that tease and dance,
Misread signs, yet here's my chance.
Who needs manuals written in prose?
I'll take the road that humor chose.

With every slip, a laugh I find,
Guided by the goof of my mind.
No heavy books to hold me down,
Just funny moments in this town.

## Tales of the Unwritten Norms

With no rulebook in my hand,
I embark on a journey unplanned.
Expectations fly, but I stay still,
Dodging life's curveballs with a thrill.

I ask the stars for advice at night,
They chuckle back, just out of sight.
Navigating chaos with a grin,
Unwritten tales where we begin.

Friendship norms seem to disappear,
When I spill secrets with a beer.
No charts or maps for this wild quest,
Just endless laughter is my guest.

Every stumble, every quirk,
Turns into gold with a little smirk.
In this wacky world, I'll make my way,
With tales of mischief, come what may.

## Seeking Wisdom in the Silence

I sat in silence, thought I'd muse,
But the sock drawer started to snooze.
Wisdom loomed, but where was it hid?
I cracked a joke, and off it slid.

Pondering life, I check the fridge,
No answers found, just a soggy lid.
A wise old sage once said to me,
"Check the pantry for recipe glee!"

In quiet moments, nonsense blooms,
Like socks and fables, chaos looms.
I seek advice from my pet goldfish,
But all he does is swish and swish.

So here I sit, with snacks in hand,
My only wisdom is from this band.
The best insights, it seems, arise,
From laughter shared with goofy ties.

## **Footprints on the Path of Wonder**

With footprints tracing paths anew,
I stumble forward, what to do?
Maps are drawn in crayon and cheer,
Exploration's fun when you steer clear!

The path gets twisty, oh what a game,
I trip on roots that tease my name.
Every scratch is a badge of pride,
With laughter echoing by my side.

Oddball encounters, they fuel my quest,
From dancing squirrels to jesters dressed.
Secrets shared with the giddy breeze,
Wonders bloom like a thousand trees.

Though the guide is lost in a cloud,
I'll navigate this goofy crowd.
With a wink and a skip, I take my aim,
For every misstep, there's joy to claim.

## The Aches of Discovery

I tripped on my shoelace, oh what a sight,
Found wisdom in bushes, but it gave me a fright.
If only a manual for all these stumbles,
Maybe I'd not have fallen in so many crumbles.

With every odd twist, I laugh through the pain,
Collecting my lessons like dogs chase the rain.
Charting my path with each silly mistake,
Seeking the guidebook, but who needs a break?

The bumps and the bruises, they add to the tale,
Like comic strips drawn with a splash of ale.
I wear my confusion like a badge that I flaunt,
Fumbling through life like a clueless old aunt.

Ask for directions? I'll give you a wink,
Turns out lost roads lead us to laugh and to think.
So here's to the journey, odd and quite wry,
Who needs an instruction book, let's just fly high!

## The Cartography of Heartbeats

My heart beats in rhythms, a curious dance,
But directions are hazy, they leave nothing to chance.
A map made of giggles and muffins galore,
Where the 'X' marks the spot for fun at the shore.

I tried to follow signs, but they all led to pie,
Navigating love feels like flying a kite.
With feelings that swirl like a kite in the air,
I scribble my journey just to be fair.

Navigators swoon with compass in hand,
But here I am lost in a wonderland.
Tracing my heartbeat on napkins and dreams,
A cartographer's chaos bursting at seams.

Each thump is a marker, each pause full of doubt,
Yet in every misstep, there's joy all about.
So here's to the laughter as hearts intertwine,
We'll map out the giggles with glittery twine!

## Unmuffled Cries for Understanding

In the theater of life, I raise up a plea,
Waving my arms loud, oh please listen to me!
With questions like popcorn, they pop and they fly,
Yet answers are quiet, they just sit and sigh.

Why is the sky blue? What's up with months late?
Why do cats think they're the masters of fate?
My voice is a chorus of comic distress,
Begging for guidance, but it's all just a mess.

I question the universe over cups of tea,
With biscuits that crumble, oh where could it be?
A wisdom-filled oracle or wisecrack-prone sage,
Will someone inform me? I'm stuck on this stage!

With every loud giggle, a tear did arise,
I'll trade all my queries for sweet, silly lies.
Who needs understanding when laughter is here?
Let's drown our confusions in giggles and cheer!

## The Code of Change and Resilience

They say change is easy, just a flick of a switch,
Yet I fumble and bumble, oh isn't it rich?
Like finding a code written just in my dreams,
I scribble and sketch, but their logic just screams.

Resilience is tough; I stumble, I tease,
Yet every fall's softer with laughter's sweet breeze.
I code my desires in rhymes that don't fit,
Like searching for rules in a wiggle-dance skit.

The world spins in circles, I spin with a grin,
Embracing the change like a true joker's kin.
With every odd challenge, I shift and I sway,
A code built on warmth is the best sort of play.

So let's jive with the chaos, dance under the moon,
With a heart full of change, we'll figure it soon.
Together we'll zigzag, and bump like a tune,
Who needs to decode when it's all just a boon?

## The Guidebook of Serendipity

In a world full of quirks and spins,
I'm searching for rules, but there are none to pin.
The coffee spills, the pies fly high,
Oh, where's the manual? I just want to try!

When I think I'm lost, I find my shoe,
Stuck to gum on the sole of my view.
A map to the future? Just look to the sky,
With clouds for guidance, I'll take to the high.

Every twist and turn feels like a game,
But wait, is that pudding? Or is it just fame?
I'll taste all the flavors this life has in store,
With a spoon in one hand, and laughter galore!

So here's to the mess and the cheery surprise,
For life's just a circus in a grand disguise.
When the rules are all missing, the fun's just begun,
With joy in my heart, I'll cherish the run!

## Understanding the Puzzles of the Heart

Hearts shaped like puzzles, and mine's missing a piece,
I ask for direction, they say, 'Try some fleece!'
With hugs as my clues, and laughter to span,
I dance through the chaos, while wearing a fan.

Do they come with instructions? Or maybe a chart?
Love can be quirky, like soup on a tart.
Each breath's a riddle, each sigh a joke,
Who knew affection could come with a poke?

Whispers of sweetness, and then there's a shout,
Do I follow the map, or seek something out?
I'll play hide and seek with feelings so bold,
While juggling emotions like diamonds and gold.

It's all a masterpiece, this work of the heart,
With each "what the heck?" a brand new start.
So let's toast to the puzzles, the laughs, and the art,
For searching for answers just propels the heart!

## The Dance of Chaos and Control

In the dance of the daffodils, chaos takes the lead,
While I trip on my shoelaces, with a cap and a bead.
The steps are all jumbled, do I spin or just sway?
A two-step, a tumble, oh what's the play today?

With partners in pandemonium, we waltz and we whirl,
In this crazy ballet, as life gives a twirl.
Sometimes we scramble to catch a quick breath,
Yet laughter erupts, like a surprise party's death.

Down the road of mayhem, I spin right and left,
With dreams as my partners, I'll grab all that's deft.
But oh, what a racket when control goes astray,
The chaos dances boldly, come dive in, hooray!

So let's jive with the blunders, embrace every fall,
For in this mad scramble, there's rhythm in all.
With a wink and a grin, let the wild swing grow,
In the dance of the rumbles, we'll steal the show!

## Embracing the Mist of Tomorrow


Tomorrow's a mystery wrapped up in a fog,
I sip my hot cocoa, while petting my dog.
With marshmallows melting, and whims in the air,
Who needs a roadmap when we've got a chair?

The mist swirls around, as thoughts start to roam,
Am I meant to wander, or just sit at home?
The sunrise is playing peek-a-boo with my mind,
Each yawn's a reminder of wonders to find.

Tick-tock says the clock, as the moments procure,
But I'll chase down the sunbeams—of that I'm sure!
With giggles as fuel, I'll paint with a brush,
Every little sunrise inspires a rush.

So here's to the mist, and the giggles it brings,
To the feathers of whimsy, on rainbow-like wings.
Tomorrow can wait, let the fog roll and play,
For what's to come next is the joy of today!

## Navigating Through the Fog

In a world of twists and bends,
I search for signs and friendly bends.
Chasing shadows, losing track,
Did I bring my map or snack?

With every turn, a crazy spin,
Forgot my keys, and where I've been.
A chuckle escapes, oh what a sight,
Is there a GPS that guides with light?

Steps on paths I've never tread,
Checking my watch, it's way past bed.
Should I laugh or should I cry?
Where's my manual? Oh my, oh my!

In this maze of oh-so-fun,
I'll whip up laughter, it's never done.
Through fog and whimsy, I will glide,
With humor as my trusty guide.

## The Book of Buried Dreams

On dusty shelves, my dreams lay low,
Some with spark, and some with woe.
I flip the pages, in search of glee,
Why can't this book just speak to me?

Lost in chapters, I trip and fall,
"Write your own!" the voices call.
But pencil's missing, so where's the fun?
Post-it notes? Just one by one.

With doodles wild, and scribbles bold,
The plot twists are a sight to behold!
I laugh aloud at each slip and turn,
In this book of dreams, I will learn!

Let's bake a cake of hopes and whims,
Serve it with laughter, on colorful rims.
For buried dreams can sprout anew,
Just grab a seat, and join the view.

## The Dance of Serendipity

Twisting, turning in a grand ballet,
Accidental leaps lead me astray.
With two left feet, I shuffle along,
Finding joy where I don't belong.

Side-stepping mishaps, a fumbled spin,
Suddenly grinning, let the fun begin!
What's the step? Who knows the score?
With serendipity, I'll dance some more.

With laughter soaring, I take a chance,
Couples of chaos, a clumsy dance.
Oh, the rhythm is often askew,
Yet in this chaos, I groove anew!

In a world where folly leads the way,
I'll dance through the night, come what may.
Embrace each misstep; let laughter unfold,
In this dance of chance, we are bold!

## Untamed Pages of Existence

I opened a book, and what a mess,
Pages flutter, no need to stress.
Some scribbles cute, some wild and free,
Each one a tale, come dance with me!

Oh what's this? A recipe gone wrong,
Add a dash of chaos, oh-so-strong!
Mix it with giggles, stir in the fun,
Bake in the sun, till the day is done.

Post-it notes and coffee stains,
Accidental joys in life's remains.
Every chapter, a rollercoaster ride,
Flip through the pages, let giggles collide!

In this book, absurdity reigns,
With untamed stories, joy sustains.
So grab your pen, let your thoughts burst,
On these wild pages, let's quench our thirst!

## Echoes from the Absent Author

I woke up this morning, oh what a surprise,
My toast invades, the jam flies through the skies.
Lost in the shuffle of missing advice,
I wonder if not knowing is part of the spice.

The cat looks at me like I've lost my head,
A purr and a nibble on yesterday's bread.
Is there a chapter on managing fur?
Or is that a quest for each new human blur?

The neighbors are shouting, a dance fills the air,
Who wrote the script for this chaotic affair?
With socks on the ceiling and hats on the floor,
I'm pretty sure fun must be hiding by the door.

So here's to the moments, a script in my hand,
While I search for the wisdom, though nobody planned.
A giggle, a shrug, let the laughter unfurl,
For who really needs rules in this whimsical whirl?

## The Spectrum of Unseen Choices

Woke up with a goal, it's breakfast I seek,
Cereal or pancakes, I feel so unique.
The fridge is a canvas, what will I create?
My stomach is eager, but the clock says, "Wait!"

I pick up a spoon, take a gamble on beans,
Taste of adventure, or was that just dreams?
A dash of good fortune and a sprinkle of fun,
Who knew that chaos could follow just one?

The path to success looks like spaghetti on plates,
Twisting and turning, like fate under crates.
With forks in the road, I chuckle and cheer,
For every misstep is a tickle, I swear!

And so I traverse this bright puzzle of fate,
Embracing the mishaps while needing a plate.
I dance through the mishmash and greet my next prey,
Tomorrow is tricky, but today's here to play!

## Mapping the Terrain of Existence

They say that my journey requires a true plan,
But I'm lost in the forest, with a lollipop can.
The map's upside down, and time's in a twist,
Where's the next landmark? I've totally missed!

A squirrel waves hello, as I chase my own tail,
Life's little surprises, like finding a snail.
With a laugh and some stumbles, I forge my own track,
Maybe it's normal, or is that just whack?

I'll climb all these mountains, or slide down with glee,
With no compass to guide, this is how it should be.
Random and wild is my favorite affair,
Just follow the giggles, I swear it's fair!

So here's to the journey, come join in the fun,
With laughter as fuel, it has just begun.
The map may be missing, but who needs a guide?
In this crazy adventure, I'll boldly abide!

## Glimpses Through the Hazy Glass

In the fog of confusion, I peer through the haze,
Searching for answers, in so many ways.
The mirror is cracked, reflections are shy,
But oh, the absurdities make me comply.

The toaster confesses its dreams in a toast,
Just trying to figure out what matters the most.
Will I party with waffles or wrestle with bread?
In this circus of choices, I follow instead.

The sun laughs at problems, with a wink and a grin,
Who knew that the paradoxes were built right in?
I throw up my hands, echoing through the mist,
Not all who wander are sightless, I insist!

Here's to the giggles, the slips, and the slides,
These glimpses of joy where the funny truth hides.
With whimsy as guide, I'll frolic along,
In this play of existence, I'll sing my own song!

## The Mystery of Unwritten Chapters

In the book of days, I find a blank,
With scribbles and doodles, all too rank.
The cover is pretty, but the pages are bare,
Where's the guide to the chaos that fills the air?

I flip through the leaves, nothing there to find,
Just random musings of an unhelpful kind.
Should I laugh or cry? I can't seem to tell,
The pages are silent, yet they scream as well.

I seek the answers but trip on a page,
Turning in circles like a circus stage.
Each chapter a riddle, each verse a ruckus,
Who needs instruction? It's all kind of funky!

With every turn, I've lost a few socks,
And learned that life's just a box of old socks.
Nudging the pages, I fumble and grumble,
But hey, at least my worries can tumble!

# Maps without Borders in a Mapless World.

I pulled out a map from a cereal box,
Directions in nonsense, it looks like a hoax.
The north is a myth, the south is a snack,
Each path leads to nowhere, all I do is yak.

I wander through streets named Thingamajig,
Crossing the bridge of a mythical pig.
Each corner bewildered, each turn a mistake,
Who knew navigation could be such a quake?

With landmarks that shift and a compass that spins,
I followed my nose, but it led to my sins.
A journey of banter, a trek of a jest,
Who needs a map when you're on a quest?

Sipping on laughter, tasting the breeze,
Every misstep's a joy, if you aim to please.
Though direction is lost, I dance in the fray,
In a world full of maps, I'll play my own way!

## Navigating the Unwritten Path

On roads that are bumpy, I trudge with a grin,
No signs pointing out where the fun will begin.
With shoes that are squeaky and socks full of holes,
I wander and wonder, embracing my foals.

I clutch at a coffee, with caramel waves,
Each sip is an adventure, my tastebud braves.
The paths are unwritten, the trails may decay,
But laughter and giggles will pave out the way.

With every misstep, oh, the joy that I find,
Like dancing on clouds, so whimsically blind.
Each stumble a story, each wiggle a cheer,
The unwritten path, my heart holds it dear.

Who needs a playbook when joy's on the rise?
With giggles and grins, I'll keep chasing the skies.
In this maze of the mad, I find all my worth,
Just follow your giggle and wander the earth!

## **Instructions on Breath and Beat**

Take a breath in, then let it be free,
Like popcorn a-popping, just let it decree.
With a twist and a turn, make beats with your feet,
Dance like no one's watching, that's quite the treat.

Now tap on your chest, give your heart some drum,
Add a sprinkle of joy—oh, isn't it fun?
Each beat is a hug, a whimsical squeeze,
With laughter enchanting the moment, it frees.

Instructions are few, but fun comes in spades,
Skip through the moments, ignore all charades.
Who needs a manual when joy lights the way?
Just breathe and keep dancing, come what may!

So skip and so sway, let the rhythm arise,
With giggles in pockets, and stars in your eyes.
Embrace every heartbeat, let happiness flow,
In a world full of wonder, just let yourself glow!

## Unraveled Threads of Existence

I searched for my guide on the shelf,
A dusty old book, or was it just myself?
Tangled in thoughts, like spaghetti on a plate,
I guess it's not too late to contemplate.

With socks that don't match, and meals burnt to black,
I wade through these quirks, feel the joy I can track.
Chasing my dreams like a cat on a fly,
Just when I trip, I can't help but sigh.

Every hiccup and stumble, a step to embrace,
Laughter is found in the silliest place.
If life's a wild ride, I forgot to install,
The seatbelt that holds me in, I guess I'll just fall.

In this circus called "me," I'm the star of the show,
With a tutu and hat, I put on a glow.
My manual's missing, but look how I thrive,
In the chaos of wonder, I'm truly alive.

## The Manual I Never Received

Woke up with coffee, was it decaf today?
Followed the scent, but lost on the way.
The toaster is hissing, and the cat wants to fight,
I'm juggling my breakfast, oh what a delight!

Instructions for how to adult? Not a clue,
But I've mastered the art of burning my stew.
With socks on my hands and a grin on my face,
Who knew silly moments could feel like a race?

I flipped through the pages, but they're all blank,
No hints for the path, I'm just stuck in a prank.
Each day's an adventure, no bookends in sight,
Guess I'm the author, and I'm loving the flight.

My life's a sitcom, the laughter is real,
With bloopers and blunders, oh what a deal!
Spilling my secrets like candy in rain,
The joy's in the mess, and who's keeping the grain?

## A Journey Without a Compass

Maps are for wanderers, I'm just here for fun,
With a wild sense of humor, I run before sun.
My enthusiasm's bright, though direction's a mess,
I'll take my own turns, I'm not here to impress.

Road signs are merely suggestions to me,
I forge my own path, come along if you see.
Every detour I take leads me further astray,
But laughter's the fuel that brightens my day.

Like a squirrel with acorns, I gather delight,
And dance through the pitfalls, oh what a sight!
Each stumble's a chance to perfect my own jig,
Guess I'll skip to the beat, I'm a no-worry twig.

In this comic mishap, I find my own cheer,
What's lost in translation is found in a year.
So here's to the chaos, the ramble and roam,
For each laugh and each fall, I'm still lucky at home.

## The Map to Hidden Joys

If only I had a guide full of zany tips,
To dodge life's pitfalls and all of its slips.
With arrows in hand, I would set off with zeal,
Searching for treasures, each laugh a fine meal.

Behind every corner, I find goofy sights,
From squirrels wearing hats to rainbow-colored tights.
Each chuckle I gather just brightens the way,
Who needs perfect plans when you can laugh and play?

I scribble my notes on the back of my hand,
With doodles and doodads, hey now, isn't it grand?
This map's a mess, but it leads to delight,
In the winks and the giggles, I'm soaring like a kite.

So here's to the journey, with or without plans,
Where joy hides in moments, and laughter expands.
The map is a riddle, come join in the fun,
Each day's a new chapter—let's see what's begun!

## **Bridges Built from Unread Tomes**

Pages piled, dust collects,
Wisdom hides in shelves like decks.
We stumble through this clumsy dance,
With footnotes lost, we take our chance.

Guided by a coffee stain,
Conversations mix like sun and rain.
We build our bridges, brick by brick,
Though none of us can read the script.

### The Orchestra of Human Experience

Instruments clash, a wild parade,
Each person plays, yet none bother to trade.
We're marching in sync, or so we believe,
But off-key notes make the heart grieve.

Conductor's lost in a sea of sighs,
As symphonies fade into awkward goodbyes.
Though we stumble, we sing with glee,
Creating tunes of chaotic unity.

## Seeking Harmony in Dissonance

Two left feet on a slippery floor,
We twirl and spin, then tumble and roar.
Chasing balance like a noble fool,
In the grand ballet of life's quirky school.

Amidst the clatter, laughter we mend,
Dissonance feels like a long-lost friend.
With every misstep, we find new grace,
In the glorious mess of this wild race.

## The Art of Serendipitous Turns

Maps await, yet we take our cue,
Wander off path, just me and you.
With no GPS, we stumble and roam,
Finding treasures in the abstract unknown.

Each corner turned reveals a surprise,
Like socks that vanish or pies in the skies.
Fortune favors the clumsy and bold,
In unexpected journeys, our stories unfold.

## The Song of Unanswered Questions

Why do socks disappear?
They vanish without a peep,
Like they joined a secret club,
While I'm left here in heap.

What's the point of my toaster?
Burnt bread is its delight,
Pop it down for breakfast bliss,
And it traps me in fright.

Why do plants need water?
Can't they just drink the air?
If they'd only share their trick,
I'd be the millionaire!

Why do we rush through each day?
And then sit stuck in cars,
While we wonder what we missed,
Counting life's missed stars.

## Embracing the Chaos of Creation

In a world of jumbled colors,
Paint drips down the floor,
I'm mixing reds and blues,
And hoping for something more.

I baked a cake for dinner;
It rose to such great heights,
But it slipped right off the counter,
And flew into the night.

My plants do yoga daily,
They stretch toward the light,
Yet here I am just stumbling,
As my limbs start to fight.

Creating without guidelines,
Is a thrilling kind of mess,
In chaos, joy finds a way,
This life, I must confess!

## Journals of Unspoken Fears

I have a book of worries,
With pages thick and bold,
Each line a wild adventure,
All my secrets to hold.

What if cows learn to fly?
And start herding us back?
Do they land with gentle hooves,
Or leave me in their track?

My pen writes all my doubts,
While I fail math with flair,
It calculates my worth,
And it's always unaware.

I scribble down my fish dreams,
In a bubble bath with glee,
They swim within the pages,
Just like they're free!

## The Road Less Traveled by Heart

I took the road less traveled,
It led me through the trees,
Where squirrels had board meetings,
And laughed at my unease.

I met a wise old turtle,
Who wore a tiny hat,
He said, 'Slow down, young traveler,
Your rush is just for that.'

At crossroads I just doodled,
With crayons bright and wide,
Mistakes turned into smiles,
As my fears took a ride.

So here's to the odd journey,
With all its bumps and turns,
We'll dance on paths uncertain,
While everyone still learns.

## Unveiling the Manuscript of Dreams

Stumbling through pages, I search with glee,
For wisdom in wonders, where could it be?
Recipes for laughter and joy at a glance,
But all I find are instructions to dance.

I opened a chapter on breakfast in bed,
Instead, all I found was a sleepy cat's head.
I flipped to the section on managing woes,
And tripped on a snicker while stepping on toes.

There's coffee for courage, and naps for the soul,
But none for my questions or ultimate goal.
With scribbles and doodles, I jotted down notes,
Turns out my manual's filled with old coats.

Perhaps the real guide is not in the text,
But rather the moments we toss and we flex,
With laughter our language and joy our best plan,
I'll script my own manual — just watch me, I can!

## The Compass of Inner Light

I bought a compass to steer through my days,
But it spins and it twirls like my thoughts in a maze.
It tells me to smile when I frown with a pout,
Perhaps I should just give that compass a shout.

Got lost on my journey, my map's just a grin,
It points to the laughter I keep tucked within.
With X marking smiles and arrows for cheer,
Why wasn't I told? My direction is clear!

The north star is winking, she leads me with grace,
Through giggles and hiccups, I'll find my own place.
The compass may falter, but my heart's steady beat,
Says wander with joy, and embrace the absurd beat.

So here's to the trips that no guidebook suggests,
To confetti of chaos and joyous mishaps,
With my compass of light, I'll head toward the fun,
In this wild, wobbly world, my journey's begun!

# Dancing with the Unexpected

I tripped on a whim and landed on chance,
With a twirl and a giggle, I started to dance.
The rhythm of chaos, a beat out of tune,
Yet somehow it sparkles like stars in June.

Invitations from mishaps to shimmy and sway,
With each awkward moment, I'll dance anyway.
A partner named 'Oops' pulls me close for a spin,
With laughter my costume and joy on my skin.

Who would've thought that surprises could bring,
Such fabulous footwork, such spontaneous fling?
A slide on banana peels, flinging my cares,
Turned my steps into laughter, my worries to pairs.

So here's to the dance floors where troubles take flight,
With a chuckle as lead and a grin oh so bright,
We'll whirl through the moments, the funny and true,
In this tango of life, there's no manual to view!

## The Melodies of Untold Struggles

There's a symphony playing in the back of my mind,
With all of life's lyrics, I struggle to find.
I picked up my pen for a sweet serenade,
But the notes just keep laughing and dance in parade.

My guitar's out of tune, the lyrics won't rhyme,
I'm jamming through chaos, but hey, it's my time!
Each stumble's a chorus, each fall is a song,
In the blanket of madness, I find where I belong.

Bringing out the humor from every mistake,
Like baking a cake that was meant to be flake.
A harmony rising from blunders, oh dear,
The music we make is the laughter we cheer.

With trumpets of troubles and pianos of glee,
I'll play all the notes of this wild melody.
So here's to the journey, a vibrant reprise,
In this chaotic symphony, humor is wise!

www.ingramcontent.com/pod-product-compliance
Lightning Source LLC
Chambersburg PA
CBHW072149200426
43209CB00051B/919